CME PROJECT

Geometry

Practice Workbook

PEARSON

Boston, Massachusetts
Glenview, Illinois
Shoreview, Minnesota
Upper Saddle River, New Jersey

13-digit ISBN 978-0-13-364433-3

10-digit ISBN 0-13-364433-2

1 2 3 4 5 6 7 8 9 10 11 10 09 08 07

Contents

Additional Practice

1. Explain the difference between parallel lines and parallel planes.

2. **a.** Draw the letters T and V as block letters.
   b. Which faces should you shade the same way?

3. Draw each flat figure as a solid figure. Shade parallel faces the same way.
   a.   **b.**   **c.**

4. Describe the planes of symmetry for each picture.
   a.   **b.**   **c.**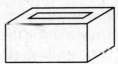

5. **a.** What is the maximum number of regions you can make in a plane using six lines? Using seven lines?
   b. Does a pattern exist to help you determine the maximum number of regions you can make in a plane based on the number of lines you use? Explain.

6. The picture represents the multiplication of two binomials.

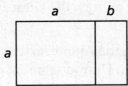

   a. What equation does the picture illustrate?
   b. Explain how this equation relates to the area of the figure.

7. Draw a picture that illustrates each equation.
   a. $(x + y)^2 = x^2 + 2xy + y^2$
   b. $(w + x)(y + z) = wy + wz + xy + xz$
   c. $x(y + z) = xy + xz$

Additional Practice

1. Suppose you follow these directions: Face south. Drive south for 2 blocks. Turn left. Drive 5 blocks. Turn left again. Drive 2 blocks. Turn left again. Drive 5 more blocks.
   a. What shape will your path form?
   b. Describe your final location. In what direction will you be facing?

2. Describe each shape by its name. Then describe each shape with a recipe that you can use to draw it.
   a.
   b.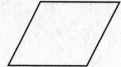
   c.

3. Read the following recipe: *Draw two parallel segments. Connect the endpoints in order.*
   a. Draw a shape the recipe describes.
   b. Can you follow this recipe to draw a different shape? Explain.

4. **a.** Draw a triangle that has only one line of symmetry.
   b. Can you draw other triangles that fit this description? What do they have in common?

5. A certain 3-dimensional solid has a vertical cross section that is a rectangle and a horizontal cross section that is a circle. Name and draw the 3-dimensional solid.

6. Write directions that describe how to draw the letters in the word CAT.

7. Draw a square. Draw a circle inside the square so that the circle touches each side of the square at one point. Draw a segment connecting the center of the circle to the bottom right corner of the square. Erase the sides of the square. What letter have you drawn?

8. Write directions that describe how to draw each figure.
   a.
   b.

Name _____ Class _____ Date _____

Additional Practice

1. Describe two ways to construct a segment that is perpendicular to a given segment.

For Exercises 2–6, use the segments below. Construct each figure using any tools necessary, other than measuring tools.

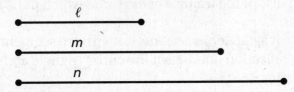

2. a square with side lengths m

3. an equilateral triangle with side lengths n

4. a trapezoid with base lengths ℓ and m

5. a nonrectangular parallelogram with side lengths m and n

6. a scalene triangle using all 3 segments

For Exercises 7–9, use the angles below. Construct each figure using any tools necessary, other than measuring tools.

7. the angle bisector of $\angle 1$

8. an angle with a measure equivalent to $m\angle 1 + m\angle 2$

9. an angle with a measure equivalent to $m\angle 2 - m\angle 1$

10. Draw a triangle on three separate pieces of paper. Use one triangle for each paper-folding construction below.
    a. Construct three medians.
    b. Construct three angle bisectors.
    c. Construct three midlines.

11. Use a compass to construct three circles that share a center. The radius of each successive circle should be twice the radius of the previous circle.

12. Describe a method to construct a square inscribed in a circle.

Additional Practice

Use the appropriate tools of a geometry software program.

1. Draw a scalene triangle and label each vertex.
   a. Move a vertex. Then move a different vertex. Which parts of the triangle change and which parts stay the same?
   b. Move a side. Which parts of the triangle change and which parts stay the same?
   c. Adjust the triangle so it again looks scalene. Construct a segment anywhere. Make it a reflection line. Select the entire triangle and reflect it. Label each new vertex.
   d. Move a vertex of the original triangle. Then move a side. What changes take place?
   e. Construct segments that connect the vertices of the original triangle to the corresponding vertices of its image. What seems to be the relationship between these segments? Does this relationship change if you move a side or an angle?

2. Draw a quadrilateral and label each vertex.
   a. Construct the midpoints of each side.
   b. Connect the midpoints to form a smaller quadrilateral. Label each of these vertices.
   c. Measure the length and the slopes of the sides of the smaller quadrilateral. What kind of quadrilateral does it seem to be?
   d. Measure the angles of the smaller quadrilateral. Do the measurements confirm your conjecture about the quadrilateral's type?
   e. Move a vertex and then move a side of the larger quadrilateral. Does your conjecture about the smaller quadrilateral remain the same?

3. Draw a triangle of any size.
   a. Construct a median of the triangle.
   b. Measure and record the lengths of the sides and the median, the measures of the angles, and the perimeter of the triangle.
   c. Change the scale of the triangle and remeasure each part in part (b).
   d. Compare the measures of the two triangles. Describe the ratios of corresponding parts.

Name _____ Class _____ Date _____

Additional Practice

Lesson 1.9

Using a compass and a straightedge, construct each UnMessUpable figure.

1. a rectangle that will always remain a rectangle

2. two circles that share a center and have radii in a ratio of 2 : 1

3. three circles that are the same size and tangent to each other

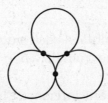

4. a. Construct a square that you can adjust in size and orientation, but that remains a square.
   b. How can you make sure that the quadrilateral you construct is a square?

5. Find two different ways to construct an equilateral triangle with geometry software. Write clear directions for each construction.

6. Construct a segment *AB*. Construct points *X* and *Y* on segment *AB* so that *AX* = *XY* = *YB*.

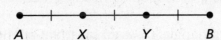

7. Construct a regular hexagon inscribed in a circle that will remain a regular hexagon as the radius of the circle changes.

Additional Practice

Use the appropriate tools of a geometry software program.

1. Construct scalene triangle ABC. Find the midpoints of $\overline{AB}$ and $\overline{BC}$.
   a. Construct $\overline{DE}$ to connect the midpoints.
   b. Measure the length of $\overline{DE}$ and the length of $\overline{AC}$. What is the relationship between the lengths of these two segments?
   c. Move vertex B. What is the effect on the relationship between the lengths of $\overline{DE}$ and $\overline{AC}$?
   d. List two other measures or relationships that are invariant as B moves.

2. Construct parallelogram $ABCD$ that can be stretched to any length or width. Which of the following are invariant?
   a. the ratio of the lengths of the opposite sides, $\frac{AB}{CD}$
   b. the perimeter of parallelogram $ABCD$
   c. the ratio of the lengths of the diagonals, $\frac{AC}{BD}$
   d. the ratio of the perimeter of parallelogram $ABCD$ to its area

3. Construct a triangle. Find the midpoints of each side.
   a. Construct the three medians of the triangle. Then measure the medians.
   b. Label the point at which the medians intersect. This point is called the *centroid* of the triangle.
   c. Construct a segment from each vertex to the *centroid*. Measure the lengths of these three segments.
   d. Move a vertex and a side of the triangle. Does an invariant relationship exist between each median and its corresponding segment that you constructed in part (c)? Explain.

4. Construct a triangle. Construct the bisector of each angle.
   a. Label the point at which the angle bisectors intersect. This point is called the *incenter* of the triangle.
   b. Construct a perpendicular segment from the *incenter* to each side of the triangle. Measure the length of each of these segments. What do you notice?
   c. Manipulate any part of the triangle. Does an invariant relationship exist between the three perpendicular segments? Explain.
   d. Make a conjecture about the *incenter* of a triangle.

Additional Practice

Use the appropriate tools of a geometry software program.

1. Randomly place six points. Connect the points with segments so that you have an arbitrary convex hexagon. Construct the perpendicular bisector of each side of the hexagon.
   a. Is there a point at which three or more perpendicular bisectors are concurrent? If not, is it possible to adjust one or more vertices to make such a point?
   b. Is it possible to adjust the vertices so that all six bisectors concur at a single point?
   c. Construct all six angle bisectors. Is it possible to adjust the vertices so that all of the angle bisectors are concurrent?

2. Construct a circle.
   a. Place six points on the circle and connect them to form an irregular hexagon.
   b. Check the perpendicular bisectors of the sides for concurrence. Do you observe any invariants? Explain.

3. Construct an arbitrary trapezoid.
   a. On one side, place an arbitrary point. Connect the point to the two opposite vertices of the trapezoid. Do the same on the opposite side.
   b. Draw the diagonals of the trapezoid. Describe a surprising collinearity.

4. Construct a triangle.
   a. Construct the three medians of the triangle.
   b. Construct the three midlines of the triangle.
   c. Are any of these six segments concurrent? Is it possible to adjust the vertices so that all six segments concur at a single point?
   d. Do you observe any invariants? Explain.

5. Is the concurrence of altitudes an invariant for triangles? Experiment with several different triangles. What do your experiments suggest?

Name _____ Class _____ Date _____

Additional Practice

Given triangle *JLK*, decide whether the following statements are *true*, *false*, or *nonsensical*.

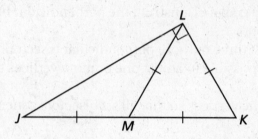

1. $m\angle KLJ = 90°$

2. $JM \cong MK$

3. $JM = MK$

4. $\angle JML \cong LMK$

5. $m\angle MJL \cong m\angle MLJ$

6. $\overline{LK} \cong \overline{LM}$

7. $m\angle LMK = m\angle LKJ$

8. $\angle J \cong \angle KLJ$

For Exercises 9 and 10, use the congruent triangles below.

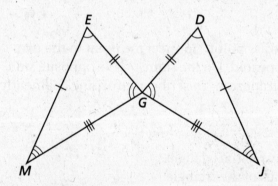

9. List all the corresponding parts.

10. Write three correct congruence statements.

11. Explain the difference between congruency and equality when comparing two figures.

12. Are all squares congruent? Explain.

13. Draw triangles *PIN* and *MAT* so that $\triangle PIN \cong \triangle MAT$. Mark congruent corresponding parts.

Additional Practice

Use the figure.

1. $\triangle ABC \cong \triangle$ _____?

2. Which congruence postulate can you use to guarantee your answer to Exercise 1?

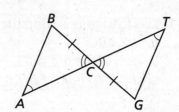

Use the figure.

3. Which pair of triangles must be congruent?

4. Which congruence postulate can you use to guarantee your answer to Exercise 3?

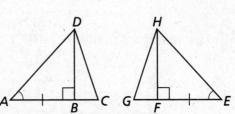

For Exercises 5–10, write a congruency statement stating which triangles are congruent. Then state which triangle congruence postulate guarantees that the triangles are congruent.

5.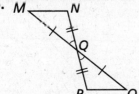

6.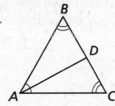

7.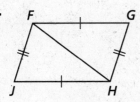

8.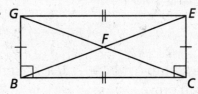

9.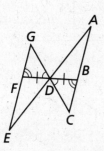

10.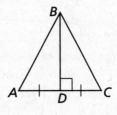

11. What does the acronym CPCTC stand for?

12. Explain why the corresponding parts AAA triplet does not prove congruency.

Additional Practice

1. Use the figure to find the measure of each angle.
   a. $m\angle EBC$
   b. $m\angle ABD$ if $m\angle CBD = 43°$
   c. $m\angle EBD$ if $m\angle CBD = 43°$

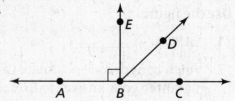

2. Use the figure to find $m\angle ABE$.

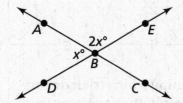

3. Use the figure to find $m\angle QRP$.

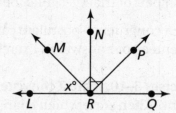

4. Below is an incomplete proof that $\angle L \cong \angle R$ in the figure. Complete the proof by providing the missing reasons.

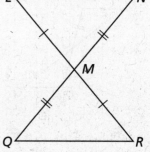

Statement	Reason
a. $\overline{LM} \cong \overline{RM}, \overline{NM} \cong \overline{QM}$	Given
b. $\angle LMN \cong \angle RMQ$	_____
c. $\triangle LMN \cong \triangle RMQ$	_____
d. $\angle L \cong \angle R$	_____

5. In the figure, $\triangle ABC \cong \triangle ADC$. List three statements you can prove.

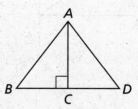

6. Given the figure, prove that $\overline{AB} \cong \overline{CB}$.

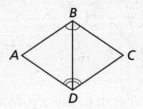

Additional Practice

1. Classify each pair of angles as *alternate interior angles, consecutive angles,* or *corresponding angles.*
  a. ∠4 and ∠2
  b. ∠3 and ∠4
  c. ∠1 and ∠5

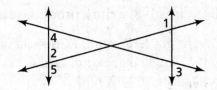

2. In the figure, $a \parallel b$.
  a. Find $m\angle 1$.
  b. Find $m\angle 2$.

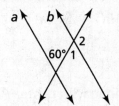

3. In the figure, $m \parallel n$ and $r \parallel s$.
  a. Which angles are congruent? Explain.
  b. Which triangles are congruent? Explain.
  c. Which segments are congruent? Explain.

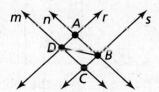

4. List the parallel lines or segments in each figure.
  a.

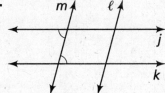

  b.

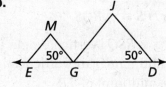

5. Find the value of x in each figure.
  a.

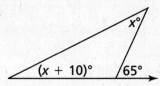

  b.

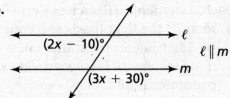

6. In the figure, H is the midpoint of both $\overline{GI}$ and $\overline{LK}$. Prove that $\overline{LG} \parallel \overline{KI}$.

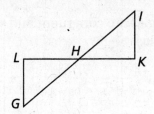

Name _____ Class _____ Date _____

Additional Practice

For Exercises 1–3, write a proof. Use a proof style described in Lesson 2.10.

1. Given: $m\angle LAB = m\angle LCB = 90°$ and $\overline{BL}$ is the
   angle bisector of $\angle ABC$.
   Prove: $\triangle LAB \cong \triangle LCB$

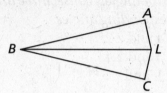

2. Given: $\overline{AB} \parallel \overline{CD}$ and $\overline{AB} \cong \overline{CD}$
   Prove: $\triangle ABC \cong \triangle CDA$

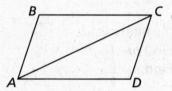

3. Given: a circle with center P and points J, K, L,
   and M on the circle
   Prove: $\triangle JKP \cong \triangle LMP$

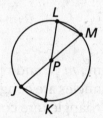

4. Describe the errors in the following proof.

   Given: S is the midpoint of $\overline{TR}$ and $\overline{PQ}$. $\angle TSP$ and $\angle RSQ$ are
   vertical angles.
   Prove: $\triangle TPS \cong \triangle RQS$

   $\therefore \angle TSP \cong \angle RSQ$ (Vertical Angle Theorem)
   $\because \angle TSP$ and $\angle RSQ$ are vertical angles.
   $\therefore S$ is the midpoint of $\overline{TR}$.
   $\therefore \overline{TS} \cong \overline{RS}$ and $\overline{PS} \cong \overline{QS}$ (definition of midpoint)
   $\therefore \triangle TPS \cong \triangle RQS$ (SAS)

For each statement in Exercises 5 and 6, follow the steps below.
   a. Identify the hypothesis and conclusion.
   b. Decide whether the statement is true or false.
   **c. If the statement is true, provide a proof. If it is false, provide a
   counterexample.**

5. An equiangular parallelogram is a square.

6. If two angles are congruent and supplementary, then both angles are
   right angles.

Additional Practice

Lessons 2.12 and 2.13

For Exercises 1 and 2, follow the steps below for each marked figure.
    a. Find the error in the "visual scan" marking.
    b. Describe an incorrect conclusion you might make as a result of
       this error.

1. Given: $\overline{LK} \cong \overline{MN}$ and $\overline{LK} \perp \overline{KN}$.

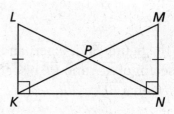

2. Given: $\overline{QS} \cong \overline{RS}$ and $\angle Q \cong \angle R$.

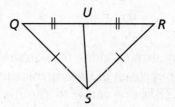

3. Make a flowchart for the proof.
    Given: $\overline{DC}$ is the perpendicular bisector of $\overline{AB}$.
    Prove: $\overline{DA} \cong \overline{DB}$

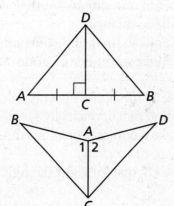

4. Use a visual scan to analyze the proof. Then
write an outline for the proof.
    Given: $\overline{AC}$ bisects $\angle BCD$, and $\angle 1 \cong \angle 2$.
    Prove: $\triangle BAC \cong \triangle DAC$

Prove each statement. Use a reverse list to write the proof.

5. If a point is on the bisector of an angle, then it is equidistant from the
sides of the angle.

6. If a point is equidistant from the endpoints of a segment, then it is on the
bisector of the segment.

7. If a triangle is a right triangle, then the acute angles are complementary.

Additional Practice

1. In the figure, *ABCD* is a rhombus.
Prove that $\overleftrightarrow{AC}$ bisects $\angle A$ and $\angle C$.

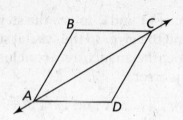

2. In the figure, $\overline{BF}$ is a perpendicular
bisector of $\overline{AC}$, and $\overline{BF}$ bisects $\angle DBE$.
Prove that $\overline{BD} \cong \overline{BE}$.

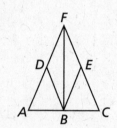

3. Cut three scalene triangles out of a piece of paper. Use one triangle
for each set of folding instructions.
   a. Fold one vertex to another vertex. Make a conjecture about the
   folded line you form.
   b. Fold one side to another side. Make a conjecture about the folded
   line you form.
   c. Fold so that a side overlaps itself and the fold contains a vertex.
   Make a conjecture about the folded line you form.

4. Use a cup or glass to trace a circle on a piece of paper. Fold the circle
in half twice, vertically and horizontally. Describe the angles you form.
Make a conjecture about the number of degrees in a circle.

Use the HL test for right triangles in each proof.

5. Given: $\triangle JKL$ is an isosceles triangle with
         base $\overline{JL}$ and $\overline{KM} \perp \overline{JL}$.
   Prove: $\triangle JKM \cong \triangle LKM$

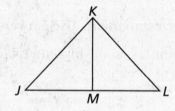

6. Given: $\overline{DH} \perp \overline{FD}$, $\overline{DH} \perp \overline{GH}$, and $\overline{FH} \cong \overline{GD}$.
   Prove: $\angle F \cong \angle G$

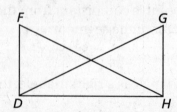

Additional Practice

For Exercises 1 and 2, use the given true statement about polygons.
   a. Describe how the statement differs from the definition of a quadrilateral.
   b. Based on the statement, are all quadrilaterals also polygons? Explain.

1. A polygon is a closed plane figure with at least three sides.

2. The sides of a polygon intersect only at their endpoints and no adjacent sides are collinear.

3. Prove that the sum of the measures of the angles of a convex quadrilateral is always 360°. Include a drawing.

4. A trapezoid is a quadrilateral with exactly one pair of parallel sides.
   a. Can a trapezoid have 2 congruent sides? 3 congruent sides?
   b. Justify your answers with examples.
   c. Can a trapezoid have exactly one right angle? Two or three right angles? Justify your answers with examples.

5. A kite is a quadrilateral in which two pairs of adjacent sides are congruent.
   a. Can a kite have 3 congruent sides? 4 congruent sides? Justify your answers with examples.
   b. Can a kite have exactly one right angle? More than one right angle? Justify your answers with examples.

6. In the figure, $\triangle ABC$ is isosceles and $\overline{BD}$ is the perpendicular bisector of $\overline{AC}$. Write an outline for a proof that $ABCD$ is a kite.

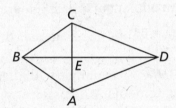

For Exercises 7–10, complete each statement with *always, sometimes,* or *never* to make the statement true. Justify your answer with a proof or examples.

7. The bases of a trapezoid are _____ congruent.

8. One diagonal of a kite _____ forms two isosceles triangles.

9. One pair of adjacent angles of a trapezoid is _____ congruent.

10. The sum of the measures of the angles of an isosceles trapezoid is _____ 360°.

Name _____ Class _____ Date _____

Additional Practice

For Exercises 1–4, use the given statement about quadrilaterals.
   a. Write the converse of the statement.
   b. Decide whether the converse is true or false.
   c. If the converse is true, provide a proof. If the converse is false, give a counterexample.

1. If a quadrilateral has opposite sides parallel, then it is a parallelogram.

2. If a quadrilateral is equiangular, then it is a parallelogram.

3. If a quadrilateral has diagonals that bisect each other, then it is a parallelogram.

4. If a quadrilateral has diagonals that are perpendicular, then it is a parallelogram.

5. In the figure, *ABCD* and *DEFG* are parallelograms. Prove each statement.
   a. $\angle B \cong \angle F$
   b. $\overline{BC} \parallel \overline{EF}$
   c. $m\angle A + m\angle F = 180°$

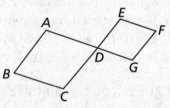

For Exercises 6–8, complete each statement with *always, sometimes,* or *never* to make the statement true.

6. A rectangle is _____ a square.

7. An equiangular parallelogram is _____ a rectangle.

8. A rhombus has diagonals that are _____ perpendicular bisectors.

9. *GHJK* is a rectangle with diagonals $\overline{GJ}$ and $\overline{HK}$. Decide whether each statement is true or false.
   a. $\angle JGH \cong \angle GJK$
   b. $\angle GKH \cong \angle JKH$
   c. $\triangle HJK \cong \triangle KGH$
   d. $\overline{GH} \parallel \overline{KJ}$

10. In the figure, *ABCD* is a rhombus. Prove that $\overline{AC} \perp \overline{BD}$.

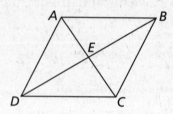

11. In the figure, *ABCD* is an isosceles trapezoid and *E, F, G,* and *H* are the midpoints of the sides. Is *EFGH* a parallelogram? Can you specify which type? Explain.

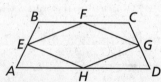

Additional Practice

1. List all the properties of a square that you can think of. Can you think of a dissection that will turn the square into an isosceles triangle? Explain.

2. Use the figure. Suppose you slide $\triangle ABD$ to the right and flip it. Explain how the properties of squares guarantee each of the following.
   a. $\overline{AB}$ fits $\overline{CD}$ exactly.
   b. The new top edge is straight.

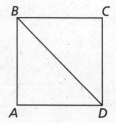

3. If you cut along the other diagonal in Exercise 2, will you get a different triangle? Explain.

4. Describe how to dissect a parallelogram into pieces that you can rearrange to form each shape.
   a. isosceles triangle
   b. right triangle
   c. trapezoid
   d. rectangle

5. In the figure, $ACDF$ is an isosceles trapezoid, B is the midpoint of $\overline{AC}$, and E is the midpoint of $\overline{DF}$. Write an outline for a proof to show that $\overline{BE} \parallel \overline{CD}$ and $\overline{BE} \parallel \overline{AF}$.

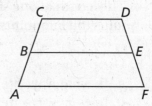

6. Write specific and clear algorithms for each dissection.
   a. triangle to rectangle
   b. parallelogram to rectangle
   c. trapezoid to rectangle

7. Find a partner. Exchange the algorithms you wrote in Exercise 6.
   a. Follow your partner's algorithms. Do the algorithms work? Are the directions clear?
   b. Give your partner feedback on the algorithms you tried. Ask your partner for feedback on your algorithms. How can you improve your algorithms?

8. Write an algorithm for one part of your daily routine, such as making your bed or brushing your teeth. Describe how your algorithm might differ from a classmate's algorithm.

Name _____ Class _____ Date _____

Additional Practice

1. A student gave the following argument for dissecting a triangle into a parallelogram.

 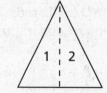 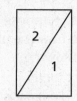

Find midpoint of base.   Move piece 2.

   a. What is wrong with this argument?
   b. For which type(s) of triangles does this dissection work?

2. **a.** Write an algorithm for dissecting an isosceles trapezoid into a rectangle.
   b. Justify each step of the algorithm.

3. **a.** Write an algorithm for dissecting a parallelogram into a triangle.
   b. Justify each step of the algorithm.

4. The length of one side of a triangle is 16. How long is the segment that joins the midpoints of the other two sides?

5. Use the figure.
   a. In what ways are $\triangle ACE$ and $\triangle BCD$ the same?
   b. In what ways are $\triangle ACE$ and $\triangle BCD$ different?
   c. Make a conjecture about $\triangle ACE$ and $\triangle BCD$.

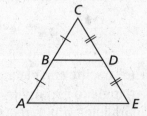

6. Use quadrilateral *ABCD*. The midpoints of the sides are *E*, *F*, *G*, and *H*. Explain why $\overline{HE}$ is congruent to $\overline{GF}$.

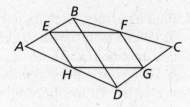

7. A kite has diagonals with lengths 10 and 18. You form a quadrilateral by joining the midpoints of the kite's sides.
   a. What is the perimeter of the inner quadrilateral?
   b. Describe the angles of the inner quadrilateral.

Additional Practice

1. Which of the following parallelograms have equal areas? Are any of the parallelograms congruent?

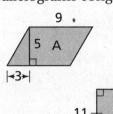

For Exercises 2–9, find the area of each figure.

2.

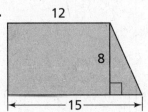

3.

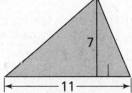

4.

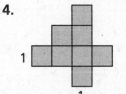

5.

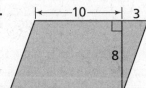

6.

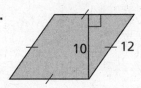

7.

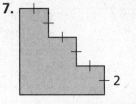

8.

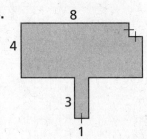

9.

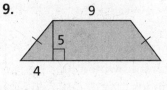

10. In square *ABCD*, is the sum of the areas of △*ADF* and △*BCF* greater than, less than, or equal to the area of △*ABF*? Justify your answer.

Name _____ Class _____ Date _____

Additional Practice

Lesson 3.8

Find the area of each figure.

1.
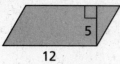
5
12

2.
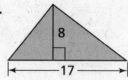
8
17

3.
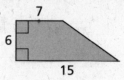
7
6
15

For Exercises 4–7, decide whether each statement is *always*, *sometimes*, or *never* true. Justify your answer with an explanation and examples.

4. If two figures are congruent, then they have equal areas.

5. The perpendicular bisector of the base of a trapezoid divides the trapezoid into two figures of equal areas.

6. The median of a triangle divides the triangle into two triangles of equal areas.

7. The area of a region is the sum of the areas of its nonoverlapping parts.

8. Refer to the shapes below. Use measurements to answer each question. Justify your answers.

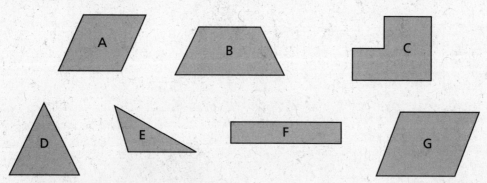

   a. Find two shapes with equal areas.
   b. List the shapes in order of areas, from least to greatest.

9. Find the area of each triangle.
   a. △FDB   b. △ABF
   c. △ABD   d. △ABC

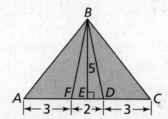

Additional Practice

Verify the Pythagorean Theorem numerically by testing a specific case.

1. Construct a right triangle with one leg 7 cm long and the other leg 24 cm long. What is the area of the triangle?

2. Construct a square with sides of length 31 cm. What is the area of the square?

3. Dissect the square in Exercise 2 into five pieces: four right triangles congruent to the triangle in Exercise 1, and one square in the middle. Find the area of the square in the middle by subtracting the areas of the four right triangles.

4. Calculate $a^2 + b^2$, or $7^2 + 24^2$. Is this sum equal to the area of the middle square in Exercise 3?

For Exercises 5–8, draw a right triangle with legs of the given lengths. Then draw a square with one side that is the hypotenuse of the triangle. Find the area and the perimeter of the square.

5. 3 cm, 4 cm

6. 6 cm, 8 cm

7. 8 cm, 15 cm

8. 9 cm, 12 cm

9. You are standing at one end of a shallow pond. There is a rectangular walking path around the pond.

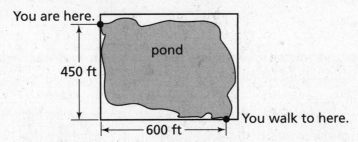

a. You walk along the path to the other end of the pond. How far do you walk?

b. You decide to wade diagonally across the pond back to your starting point. How much shorter or longer is this method than walking on the path?

A triangle has sides of the given lengths. Decide whether each triangle is a right triangle. Explain.

10. 6, 7, 12

11. 9, 40, 41

12. 3, 8, 11

Additional Practice

1. Find the length of the hypotenuse of an isosceles right triangle with legs of each given length.

   a. 2 in.   **b.** 4 in.   **c.** 5 in.   **d.** 13 in.   **e.** s

2. Find a pattern in the hypotenuse lengths you found in Exercise 1. Write a rule that relates the leg lengths of an isosceles right triangle to the length of its hypotenuse.

3. The figure is a rectangular box with the given dimensions. Find d, the length of the diagonal.

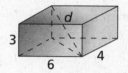

4. A triangle has side lengths 4, $4\sqrt{3}$, and 8.

   a. Numerically show that the triangle is a right triangle.

   b. Would you consider these lengths a Pythagorean triple? Explain.

For Exercises 5 and 6, find the area of each triangle.

5.

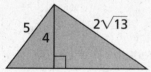

6.

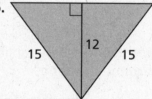

7. a. Find a Pythagorean triple not mentioned in Lesson 3.11.

   b. List four triples that would be members of its family.

8. A car drives due north for 4 miles. It turns right and drives due east for 3 miles. Then it turns right again and drives due south for 8 miles.

   a. How far is the car from its starting point?

   b. Describe a situation that might require this route, rather than a direct route from start to finish.

9. The radius of a regular hexagon is the measure from its center to any vertex. The radius is congruent to each side. Find the area of a regular hexagon with side lengths of 10.

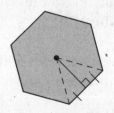

Additional Practice

Find the lateral and total surface areas for each figure.

1.
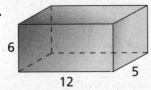
6
12
5

2.

10
4 3

3.
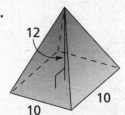
12
10
10

4.
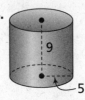
9
5

5.
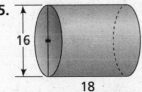
16
18

6.
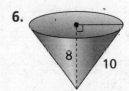
8
10

For Exercises 7–10, find the total surface area of each polyhedron with the given dimensions. Assume each polyhedron is right and regular.

7. a square prism: height 12 cm, base area 25 cm^2

8. a triangular prism: base side length 12 in., height 14 in.

9. a square pyramid: base side length 10 in., height 4 in.

10. a triangular pyramid: base side length 5 m, slant height 13 m

11. A triangular prism has base side lengths 4 cm, 5 cm, and 6 cm. The lateral surface area is 300 cm^2. What is the height of the prism?

12. The lateral surface area of a square pyramid is 240 ft^2. A base side length is 12 ft. What is the height of the pyramid?

13. The lateral surface area of a cone is 48π in.^{2}. The radius is 8 in. What is the slant height of the cone?

Additional Practice

For Exercises 1–6, find the volume of each figure.

1.

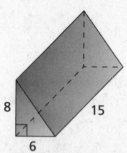

8   15   6

2. |←14→|

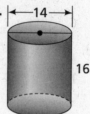

16

3.

8   17

4.

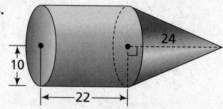

10   24   22

5.

8 10 8 10

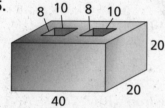

20   20   40

6.

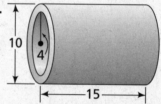

10   4   15

7. A regular square pyramid has height 15 m and volume 1815 m³. What is the length of a base side?

8. A cylindrical water tower holds 100,000π cubic feet of water. The diameter of the tower is 100 feet. What is the height of the tower?

9. A cone fits inside a cylinder so that they share a base and have the same height. The radius of the base is 4 in. and the height of the cylinder and cone is 13 in. What is the volume of air between the cone and cylinder?

10. A farmer builds a rectangular storage shed large enough to hold 1000 bales of hay. A bale of hay is 4 ft by 2 ft by 1 ft.
   a. What is total volume of hay in 1000 bales?
   b. The base of the shed is 50 ft by 20 ft. What minimum shed height, floor to ceiling, allows the farmer to store 1000 bales?

11. The diameters of two water pipes of the same length are 6 in. and 8 in. A single pipe of the same length replaces the two pipes. The single pipe has the same volume as the two original pipes combined. What is the diameter of the new pipe?

Additional Practice

Lessons 4.2 and 4.3

Decide whether the two scale factors are the same or different.

1. $\frac{3}{4}$ and 0.75   **2.** 3.5 and 35%   **3.** $\frac{3}{2}$ and $\frac{2}{3}$ **4.** 6 and 600%

Scale a rectangle that has width 18 inches and length 30 inches by each scale factor. Determine the dimensions of the scaled rectangle.

5. 2   **6.** $\frac{2}{3}$ **7.** 25%   **8.** $\frac{5}{8}$

For each pair of figures, find the scale factor that you can apply to figure X to get figure Y. Then find the scale factor that you can apply to figure Y to get figure X.

9.
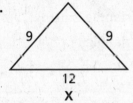

10.
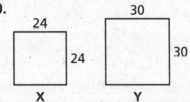

You want to convince someone that the pairs of figures below are well-scaled copies of each other. Name at least four pairs of measurements on the two figures that you could use.

11.

12.

For Exercises 13 and 14, use graph paper to scale the figures by the given scale factor.

13.
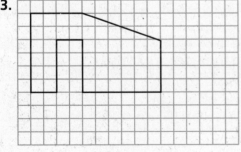

scale factor = 1.5

14.
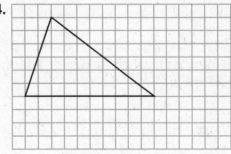

scale factor = 0.5

Name _____ Class _____ Date _____

Additional Practice

Two rectangles are scaled copies of each other. The ratio of the length of one rectangle to the length of the other is $\frac{4}{5}$. The width of the smaller rectangle is given. Find the width of the larger rectangle.

1. 20   **2.** 12   **3.** 18   **4.** 10   **5.** 6   **6.** 11

The length of a side of a scaled square is given. The scale factor is 1.5. Find the length of a side of the original square.

7. 3   **8.** 15   **9.** 1   **10.** 21   **11.** 78   **12.** 2

Use the side lengths of the two triangles to decide whether the triangles are scaled copies. Explain.

13. Triangle A: 5, 6, 10   **14.** Triangle C: 8, 12, 7   **15.** Triangle E: 10, $3\frac{1}{2}$, $7\frac{1}{2}$
     Triangle B: 10, 11, 15   Triangle D: 21, 24, 36   Triangle F: 12, 4, 9

Draw a figure inside the original figure that is a scaled copy. (You choose the scale factor.) Explain how to do it.

16.

17.

You scale a polygon by each factor. Find (a) the ratio of the lengths of any two corresponding sides of the original polygon to the scaled one, and (b) the ratio of the measures of any two corresponding angles of the original polygon to the scaled one.

18. $\frac{8}{5}$ **19.** 7   **20.** 5.4   **21.** 0.9   **22.** $\frac{3}{5}$ **23.** 1

Use the angle measures to decide whether the two triangles are scaled copies. Explain.

24. Triangle G: 45°, 45°   **25.** Triangle J: 133°, 11°   **26.** Triangle M: 55°, 82°
     Triangle H: 45°, 90°   Triangle K: 35°, 11°   Triangle N: 43°, 55°

27. Triangle P: 79°, 81°   **28.** Triangle R: 102°, 53°   **29.** Triangle V: 139°, 5°
     Triangle Q: 81°, 20°   Triangle S: 25°, 53°   Triangle W: 26°, 139°

Addtional Practice

Trace each figure, including the center of dilation. Dilate each figure by the factor 2.

1.

2.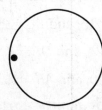

For each pair of figures, locate the center of dilation.

3.

4.

Use the figure for Exercises 5 and 6. Use a ruler to help you calculate each scale factor.

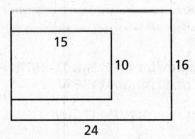

5. What is the scale factor when the dilated rectangle is the smaller one? Describe how to find the scale factor using measurement.

6. What is the scale factor when the dilated rectangle is the larger one? Describe how to find the scale factor using measurement.

From the given description, decide whether the original figure or the dilated figure is closer to the center of dilation.

7. The center of dilation is outside the original figure. You dilate the original figure by the scale factor $\frac{5}{8}$.

8. The center of dilation is outside the original figure. You dilate the original figure by the scale factor 4.

9. The center of dilation is inside the original figure. You dilate the original figure by the scale factor 9.

10. The center of dilation is inside the original figure. You dilate the original figure by the scale factor $\frac{1}{2}$.

Additional Practice

Use the figure for Exercises 1–10. In Exercises 1–9, $\overline{DE}\|\overline{BC}$.

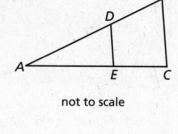

not to scale

1. When $AD = 15$, $DB = 9$, and $AE = 10$, what is EC?

2. When $AE = 18$, $EC = 12$, and $BC = 20$, what is DE?

3. When $AD = 9$, $BC = 24$, and $DE = 8$, what is AB?

4. When $AD = 8$, $AE = 10$, and $AB = 15$, what is AC?

5. When EC is half of AE, and $DE = 2.4$, what is BC?

6. When EC is 1.5 times AE, and $BC = 60$, what is DE?

7. When $DE = 12$, $BC = 15$, and $AC = 24$, what is EC?

8. When $AD = 14$ and $BD = 21$, what is the value of $\frac{DE}{BC}$?

9. When $AD = 15$, $AE = 12$, and $EC = 10$, what is the value of $\frac{BC}{DE}$?

10. Suppose you do not know whether $\overline{DE}\|\overline{BC}$, but you do know that $AD = 24$, $AC = 48$, $AE = 18$, and $DB = 40$. Is $\overline{DE}\|\overline{BC}$? Explain.

Use the figure for Exercises 11–19. In Exercises 11–18, $\overline{ST}\|\overline{UV}$, $\overline{UV}\|\overline{QR}$, and $\overline{ST}\|\overline{QR}$.

11. When $PS = 9$, $PU = 17$, and $TV = 6$, what is PT?

12. When $PS = k$, $SU = 10$, $TV = 15$, and $UQ = 18$, what is VR?

13. When $PS = 90$, $SU = 18$, and $PT = 110$, what is TV?

14. When $UV = 32$, $PV = 44$, and $PT = 8$, what is ST?

15. When $PS = 6$, $SU = 7$, $UQ = 8$, and $TR = 21$, what is PR?

16. When $PT = 7$ and $TR = 21$, what is the value of $\frac{ST}{QR}$?

17. When $SQ = 50$, $QU = 30$, and $VR = 25$, what is the value of $\frac{TV}{VR}$?

18. Is $\frac{PS}{PT} = \frac{PQ}{PR}$? Explain.

19. Suppose you do not know whether $\overline{ST}\|\overline{UV}$, $\overline{UV}\|\overline{QR}$, or $\overline{ST}\|\overline{QR}$, but you do know that $\frac{TV}{SU} = \frac{VR}{UQ}$. Which segments are parallel?

Additional Practice

In Exercises 1–9, $\overline{AB} \parallel \overline{DE}$.

Find the indicated length.

1.

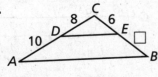

2.

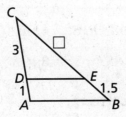

3.

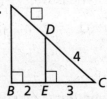

Find as many lengths as you can.

4.

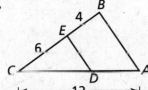

5.

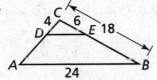

6.

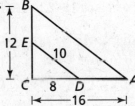

Find BC.

7.

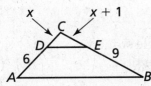

8.

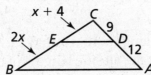

9.

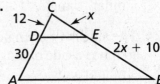

For Exercises 10–12, use the given lengths to decide whether $\overline{AB} \parallel \overline{DE}$.
Explain. (The figures are not necessarily drawn to scale.)

10.

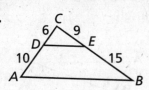

11.

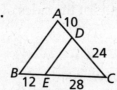

12.

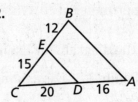

13. In $\triangle ABC$, $AB = 6$, $BC = 8$, and $AC = 9$. Point X lies on $\overline{BC}$ so that $BX = 2$.
Point Y lies on $\overline{BA}$ so that $\overline{XY} \parallel \overline{CA}$. Find BY.

Name _____ Class _____ Date _____

Additional Practice

Use the figure for Exercises 1–14. $\triangle PQS \sim \triangle RPS$.
$m\angle Q = 56°$, $m\angle PRS = 87°$, $PQ = 36$, $QS = 60$,
and $RP = 30$.

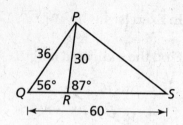

Find each measure.

1. $m\angle PRQ$ 2. $m\angle QPR$ 3. $m\angle RPS$ 4. $m\angle QPS$

5. $m\angle S$ 6. PS 7. RS 8. QR

Decide whether each statement is correct.

9. $\triangle PSQ \sim \triangle RSP$ 10. $\triangle PRS \sim \triangle QPS$ 11. $\triangle RPS \sim \triangle SQP$

12. $\triangle SQP \sim \triangle SPR$ 13. $\triangle QSP \sim \triangle RSP$ 14. $\triangle SQP \sim \triangle SPR$

In Exercises 15–22, $\triangle FAR \sim \triangle TEH$. Complete each statement.

15. $\dfrac{FR}{TH} = \dfrac{AF}{\square}$ 16. $\dfrac{EH}{TE} = \dfrac{\square}{FA}$ 17. $\dfrac{\square}{RA} = \dfrac{HT}{HE}$

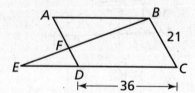

18. $\angle A \cong \square$ 19. $\angle T \cong \square$ 20. $\angle H \cong \square$

21. $\triangle ARF \sim \square$ 22. $\triangle ETH \sim \square$

23. The sides of a triangle have lengths 5, 6, and 8. A triangle similar
    to it has a side of length 10. Write all side lengths of each possible
    similar triangle.

24. The sides of a triangle have lengths 12, 18, and 18. A triangle similar
    to it has a side of length 8. Write all side lengths of each possible
    similar triangle.

25. A triangle has sides of length 5, 7, and 8. A triangle similar to it has a
    perimeter of 15. What are the lengths of the sides of this triangle?

26. A triangle has sides of length 9, 12, and 15. A triangle similar to it has a
    perimeter of 40. What are the lengths of the sides of this triangle?

Use the diagram for Exercises 27–29.

27. Figure $ABCD$ is a parallelogram. Prove that
    $\triangle ABF \sim \triangle DEF$.

28. Suppose $m\angle E = 20°$ and $m\angle C = 60°$.
    Find the measure of each angle.
    a. $\angle EBA$ b. $\angle A$ c. $\angle EDF$

29. Is $\triangle ABF \sim \triangle CEB$? Explain.

Additional Practice

1. A side of a triangle has length 9. The altitude to that side has length 16. When you make a new triangle for which you double the lengths of all the sides of the original triangle, what is the area of the new triangle?

In Exercises 2 and 3, the ratio of the areas of two rectangles is $\frac{9}{16}$.

2. If the smaller rectangle has width 27 cm, what is the width of the larger rectangle?

3. If the larger rectangle has width 27 cm, what is the length of the smaller rectangle?

4. Rachel mows a yard 150 ft by 220 ft in 1.5 hours. At that rate, how long does it take her to mow a yard that is 300 ft by 440 ft?

5. A plot of land that is 360 ft by 242 ft can produce 44 bushels of wheat. Robert purchases a plot of land that is 540 ft by 363 ft. How many bushels of wheat can his land produce?

6. A blue square has an area that is 18 times the area of a red square. What is the ratio of the length of a side of the blue square to the length of a side of the red square?

7. The area of a triangle is 72 square inches. The area of a similar triangle is 16 square inches. What is the ratio of the height of the original triangle to the height of the similar triangle?

8. A colt's paddock has an area of 300 square feet. The colt is growing, and his owner wants to scale the paddock dimensions by the factor 3.5. What is the area of the new paddock?

9. You scale a triangle by the factor 20. What is the ratio of the area of the scaled triangle to the area of the original one?

10. A rectangle has an area of 126 square inches. When you scale the lengths of the sides by the factor $\frac{2}{3}$, what is the area of the new rectangle?

11. You increase the width of a rectangle by the factor 4. You decrease the length by the factor 4. What is the ratio of the area of the new rectangle to the area of the original rectangle? Explain.

12. You increase the height of a triangle by the factor 8. The length of the base stays the same. What is the ratio of the area of the new triangle to the area of the original triangle? Explain.

13. You decrease the length of a rectangle by the factor $\frac{5}{8}$. By what factor should you change the width so that the area of the new rectangle is the same as that of the original rectangle? Explain.

14. You increase the lengths of the sides of a cube by the factor 1.5. What is the ratio of the volume of the new cube to that of the original? Explain.

Additional Practice

1. Draw a circle of radius 2 inches. Approximate its area using each of the following mesh sizes.

    a. $\frac{1}{2}$ in.   **b.** $\frac{1}{4}$ in.   **c.** $\frac{1}{8}$ in.   **d.** $\frac{1}{16}$ in.

2. How do the areas of the two circles compare?
    a. A circle of radius 4 is scaled to a circle of radius 8.
    b. A circle of radius 4 is scaled to a circle of radius 1.

3. a. Draw a circle. Inscribe an equilateral triangle in the circle and circumscribe an equilateral triangle around the circle. Calculate the perimeters of both triangles.

    b. Using the same circle, inscribe a regular hexagon in the circle and circumscribe a regular hexagon around the circle. Calculate the perimeters of both hexagons.

    c. Using the same circle, inscribe a dodecagon (12-gon) in the circle and circumscribe a dodecagon around the circle. Calculate the perimeters of both dodecagons.

    d. Use the data from parts (a)–(c) to give an approximation for the perimeter of your circle.

4. a. Draw a blob. Estimate its area using a mesh of $\frac{1}{2}$ in. Estimate the same blob's area using a mesh of $\frac{1}{4}$ in.

    b. Draw the original blob scaled by a factor of 3. Estimate the new blob's area using a mesh of $\frac{1}{2}$ in. and $\frac{1}{4}$ in.

    c. A blob and its grid of squares is scaled. Explain the relationship of the areas of both shapes.

5. Use linear approximation to estimate the following distances.
    a. the perimeter of a lake

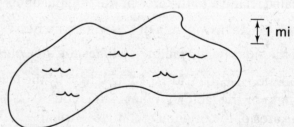

    b. the length of a cross-country running course

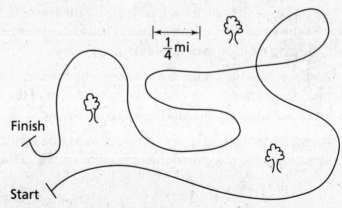

Name _____ Class _____ Date _____

Additional Practice

Lesson 5.3

1. Find the area of the following figures.

a.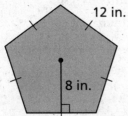
12 in.

8 in.

b.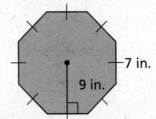
7 in.

9 in.

c.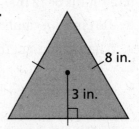
8 in.

3 in.

2. A town is planning a circular walkway that will be 2 meters wide. The walkway will have an inner radius of 5 meters with a circumference of about 31.4 meters. Find the area of the walkway.

3. A regular hexagon is inscribed in a circle of radius 4 inches.
  a. Find the area of the hexagon.
  b. Find the area that lies between the hexagon and circle.

4. A square with side length 10 cm is inscribed in a circle.
  a. Find the radius of the circle.
  b. Find the area of the circle if its circumference is 69.7 cm.

5. Find the area of an equilateral triangle inscribed in a circle with a radius of 5 in.

6. Find the area of a regular octagon with a perimeter of 96 m and an apothem of 5 m.

7. The circle in the figure has a radius of 3 in. Find the area of the shaded region.

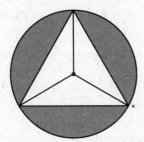

8. A bicycle's tires have a radius of 13 inches. How far does the bike travel when the tires rotate exactly 3 times?

Additional Practice

1. Find the area of a circle with the given dimensions.
   a. a radius of 12 m   **b.** a diameter of 20 in.   **c.** a radius of 8 in.

   d. the circle obtained by scaling a circle of radius 4 in. by a factor of $\frac{1}{2}$

2. **a.** What fraction of the circle's area is the shaded sector?
   b. What is the *exact* area of the circle?
   c. What is the *exact* area of the sector?

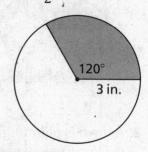

3. Find the area of each shaded region.

   a. 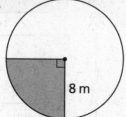   **b.** 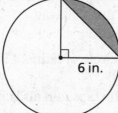   **c.**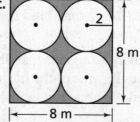

4. A pizza is cut into 6 equal slices. Find the area of one slice if the pizza has the given diameter.
   a. 12 inches   **b.** 16 inches
   c. The crust is 1 inch wide. What is the area of the slice, minus the crust, for the 12-inch pizza?

5. A "sunburst" window found above residential doorways is a half circle with five equal sectors. The window has a width of 36 inches.
   a. What is its area?
   b. What is the area of one sector of the window?

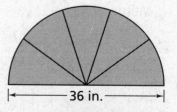

6. A rectangular pool is inscribed within a circle. A patio surrounds the pool, indicated by the shaded region. Find the area of the patio.

7. An archery target has 4 concentric circles. Each section is 3 inches wide. What is the area of the shaded section?

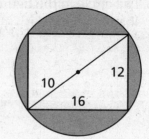

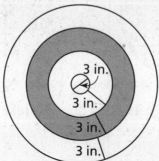

Additional Practice

1. Given a circle with the following dimensions, find its circumference.
   a. a radius of 5 m   **b.** a diameter of 12 in.   **c.** an area of 49π cm^2

2. Compare the circumferences of two circles, one with a radius of 1 inch and the other with a radius of 2 inches. Is the ratio of the diameter to the circumference the same for both circles?

3. Use a circle of radius 4 cm.
   a. Draw a sector of 90°. Find the length of each arc the sector has formed.
   b. Draw a sector of 120°. Find the length of each arc the sector has formed.

4. The table at the right gives one piece of information about four different circles. For each circle, find the missing parts.

Radius	Diameter	Area	Circumference
8			
	8		
		8	
			8

5. The circumference of a circle is 144π m.
   a. Find the radius of the circle.   **b.** Find the arc length of a 60° sector.

6. Find the length of the arc shown on each circle.
   a. 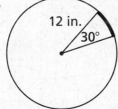   **b.** 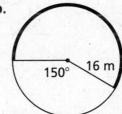   **c.**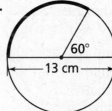

7. Find the perimeter of the shaded region. The outer square has a side of 16 cm.

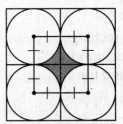

8. In one revolution, how much farther does a point 12 in. from the center of a tire travel than a point 4 in. from the center?

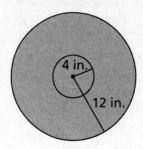

Additional Practice

1. What are the following elements called with respect to the circle?
   a. $\overline{MO}$ b. $\overline{MQ}$ c. $\overline{MN}$ d. $\angle MON$ e. $\overset{\frown}{PQ}$

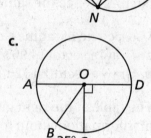

2. Draw a circle of radius 2 cm.
   a. Draw a central angle, $m\angle AOC = 60°$.
   b. Draw $\triangle AOC$. Find its height.

3. Find the measure of central angle AOB.

   a. 290°

   b. 140°

   c.

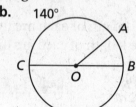

4. Given: Circle A
   Prove: $\overline{BC}\|\overline{DE}$

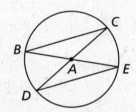

5. Find $m\angle ABC$.

   a.

   b.

   c.

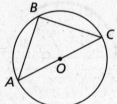 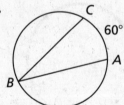

6. Find the values of the variables x, y, and z in the diagram.

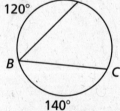

7. An equilateral triangle JLK is inscribed in a circle. If M and N are midpoints of the arcs $\overset{\frown}{LK}$ and $\overset{\frown}{KJ}$, what type of quadrilateral is $JNML$?

8. Use the diagram of a regular pentagon inscribed in a circle.
   a. What is the relationship between $m\angle 1$ and $m\angle 2$? Justify your answer.
   b. Find $m\angle 1$ and $m\angle 2$.

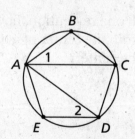

9. If two chords of a circle are parallel, prove that the two arcs between the chords are congruent.

Additional Practice

1. Draw a circle with radius 1 inch.
   a. Place a point A outside the circle. Construct two tangents to the circle, marking the points of tangency as C and D.
   b. Place a point B inside the circle. Construct two secants through point B to points C and D.

2. a. Draw a circle with perpendicular radii $\overline{AO}$ and $\overline{BO}$. Draw tangents to the circle at A and B.
   b. If the tangents meet at point C, what kind of figure is $OACB$? Write a proof to justify your answer.

3. Find the values of x and y.
   a.
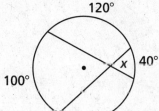
   b.
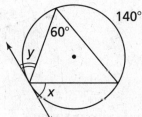
   c.
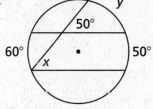

4. $\overline{OC}$ is the perpendicular bisector of tangent $\overline{AB}$. Prove that $\overset{\frown}{DC} \cong \overset{\frown}{EC}$.

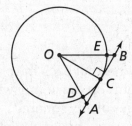

5. In the figure, Circle A and Circle B share a common tangent $\overline{CD}$. Prove that $\triangle ACE \sim \triangle BDE$.

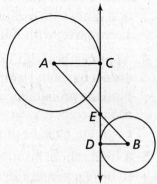

6. The power of a point P with respect to a circle is 128. A chord $\overline{JK}$ contains P such that $PK = 16$ in. Find JK.

7. The power of a point P with respect to a circle is 108. Two chords $\overline{LM}$ and $\overline{NQ}$ contain P such that $LP = 12$ and $NQ = 31$. Find PM, NP, and QP.

8. Find the value of x and state the power of point P with respect to each circle. Figures are not to scale.
   a.
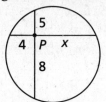
   b.
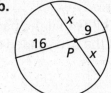

Additional Practice

1. What is the probability that a dart will land in the shaded areas of the following dartboards?

   a.
   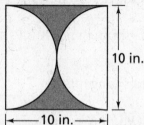
   10 in.
   10 in.

   b.
   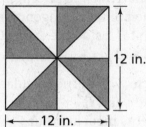
   12 in.
   12 in.

   c.
   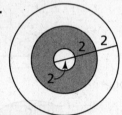

   d.
   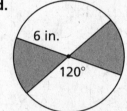
   6 in.
   120°

2. The image shows a lid of a child's shape sorter toy. A tiny drop of water falls toward the lid. What is the probability of the drop going through each given hole.
   a. the circular hole
   b. the square hole
   c. the triangular hole

   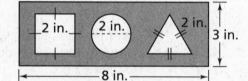
   2 in.   2 in.   2 in.
   3 in.
   8 in.

3. A checkerboard is made of 100 squares that each have a side of 30 mm. If you drop each of the following coins on the board, what is the probability that the coin will not touch any edges of any square?
   a. a dime with radius 9 mm
   b. a nickel with radius of 12 mm
   c. a quarter with radius of 15 mm

4. A spinner has with 12 equal sectors. Six of the sectors are white, and the others are each painted a different color: red, orange, yellow, green, blue, and purple. Find the probability of the wheel landing on the following sectors.
   a. any color except white
   b. red
   c. green, blue, or purple

5. A high school homecoming committee decides to have a parachutist land on the emblem of the football field during the game's half time show.
   a. What is the probability that the parachutist will land on target?
   b. What is the probability that the parachutist will land in one of the two shaded end zones?

   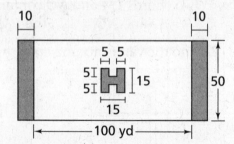
   10   10
   5 5
   5I   H   I15   50
   5I
   15
   100 yd

Additional Practice

1. What is the probability of a tiny drop (so small that it has no area) landing on a squiggly line on this board if each of the lines shown is an idealized line with no width? Why?

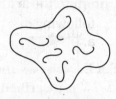

2. What is the probability of a tiny drop landing in each of the square regions: S_1, S_2, S_3, and S_4? The board is a square with side length 10 cm. Each interior region has its vertices at the midpoint of the sides of the previous larger region.

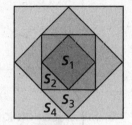

3. A spinner in a child's game has a needle with negligible width and perfect lines separating each region. What is the probability that a child will have to re-spin because he is unable to determine in which region the spinner lands?

4. At a carnival, Jeff throws darts at this dartboard. Find the probability that Jeff will score the following points with one dart.
   a. 50 points   b. 10 points   c. 30 points

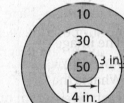

5. At a school's fundraiser, a dunk tank has a circular target with a 16-in. diameter. If a baseball is randomly thrown at the target, it must hit the exact center of the target to activate the release of the person into the tank.
   a. In this situation, does the center of the target have some measure or is it an idealized center?
   b. What is the probability of the ball hitting the center of the target if the "center" for release is 2 inches in diameter?

6. a. What is the probability that a coin of radius 8 mm will land touching all five shaded regions?
   b. If the lines between the regions are idealized lines and the coin is replaced by a tiny drop, does this change the probability in part (a)? Why?

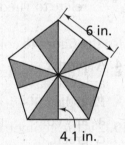

7. Use the diagram of the equilateral triangles. Each interior triangle has a side length half the length of the larger triangle. The midpoint of the base of each triangle is point P. What is the probability of a tiny drop landing in the following regions?
   a. A b. B c. C

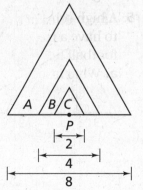

Additional Practice

Compute the arithmetic and geometric means of each pair of numbers.

1. 5 and 20

2. 8 and 16

3. 4 and 9

For Exercises 4 and 5, find the unknown segment lengths. Imagine that △JLK is inscribed in a circle.

4.
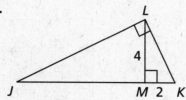

5.
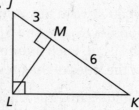

6. Suppose you know the width a and length b of one rectangle, and length c of a second rectangle.
 a. Explain how to find the width of the second rectangle so that both rectangles have the same area.
 b. Suppose the rectangbles have the same areas. If the first rectangle has dimensions 8 and 12, what is the width of the second rectangle if its length is 24?

7. Use the diagram of △ABC.
 a. Prove △ABC ~ △ADC ~ △CDB.

 b. Prove $\frac{AD}{CD} = \frac{CD}{BD}$.

 c. Prove $\frac{AB}{AC} = \frac{AC}{AD}$ and $\frac{AB}{BC} = \frac{BC}{BD}$.

 d. How do your proofs in parts (a)–(c) relate to Theorems 6.1 and 6.2?

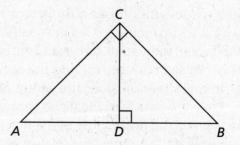

Use the figure to complete each statement.

8. x is the geometric mean of _____ and _____.

9. y is the geometric mean of _____ and _____.

10. z is the geometric mean of _____ and _____.

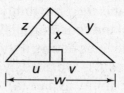

Find the values of the variables.

11.
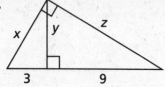

12.
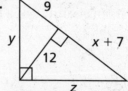

Additional Practice

For each given type of triangle, draw the three medians. Then mark the point of concurrence.

1. acute   2. obtuse   3. right

For each given type of triangle, draw the three altitudes. Mark the point of concurrence.

4. acute   5. obtuse   6. right

For each given type of triangle, draw the three angle bisectors. Then mark the point of concurrence.

7. acute   8. obtuse   9.   right

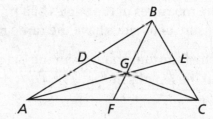

For Exercises 10–12, use $\triangle ABC$ where $\overline{AE}$, $\overline{CD}$, and $\overline{BF}$ are medians.

10. If $FB = 12$, find FG.

11. If $GC = 10$, find DC.

12. If $GE = x$, find AE.

13. What type of triangle has three medians that are also the altitudes and the angle bisectors? Justify your answer with a diagram.

14. Prove that the medians drawn to the legs of an isosceles triangle are congruent.

15. Given: Right $\triangle JLK$; $\overline{AB}$ is the perpendicular bisector of $\overline{LK}$.
Prove: $\overline{LA}$ is a median.

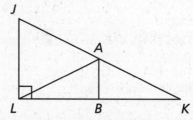

16. Draw right scalene $\triangle ABC$ with right $\angle C$. Then draw median $\overline{CD}$ from $\angle C$ to $\overline{AB}$.
    a. Which segments appear to be congruent to median $\overline{CD}$?
    b. Draw midline $\overline{DE}$. Are there any congruent triangles in your drawing? Prove your answer.
    c. Are there any similar triangles in your drawing? Prove your answer.

Name _____ Class _____ Date _____

Additional Practice

For Exercises 1–3, find any missing angle measures and side lengths.

1.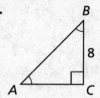

2.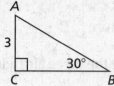

3.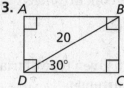

4. Use $\triangle JKL$ below. Express the lengths of $\overline{JK}$, $\overline{KL}$, $\overline{JM}$, and $\overline{ML}$ in terms of s.

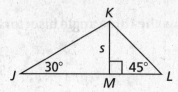

5. If the measures of the angles of a triangle have a ratio of $1 : 2 : 3$, will the measure of its sides have the same ratio? Explain.

6. Each of the four triangles in the diagram below is a 45-45-90 triangle. Find the lengths of $\overline{SW}$, $\overline{TW}$, $\overline{UW}$, and $\overline{VW}$.

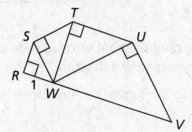

For Exercises 7–12, use $\triangle ABC$. Find each exact value.

7. $\sin A$ 8. $\cos A$

9. $\tan A$ 10. $\sin B$

11. $\cos B$ 12. $\tan B$

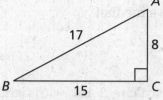

13. An airplane flies in a straight line at an altitude of 10,000 feet. The plane begins its descent toward the airport, making an angle of 3° with its straight flight path.
   a. To the nearest foot, how far will the plane fly to reach the airport?
   b. To the nearest foot, how far in ground distance is the plane from the airport when it begins its descent?

14. A 30-foot ladder is leaning against a house. The ladder makes a 40° angle with the ground. To the nearest tenth of a foot, how high up the side of the house is the top of the ladder?

Additional Practice

Find all the missing side lengths and angle measures for each triangle.

1.
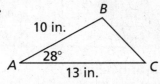

2.
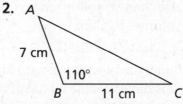

3.
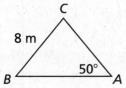

4.
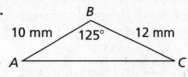

Use the figure and the given information to find the missing side lengths and angle measures of △ABC.

5. The area of △ABC is exactly 33 in.², $AD = 6$ in., and $DC = 9$ in.

6. The area of △ABC is exactly 64 m², $AC = 16$ m, and $BD = 6$ m.

7. The area of △ABC is exactly 72 cm², $BD = 12$ cm, and $m\angle A = 70°$.

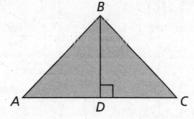

Find the length of the third side.

8.
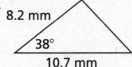

9.
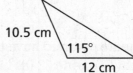

Find the measure of ∠A.

10.
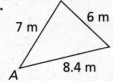

11.
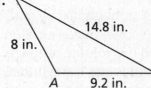

Find the area of the triangle.

12.
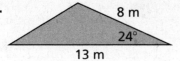

13.
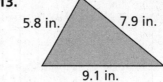

Additional Practice

1. You can deform a right cylinder as shown. Do the two solids have the same volume? Explain.

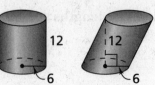

2. A right cylinder and a square prism have the same volume and height.
   a. Both solids have volume 60 m³. If the cylinder has radius 3 m, find the area of the base of the prism.
   b. If the base of the prism has side length 8 cm, find the radius of the cylinder.

For Exercises 3–6, find the volume of each solid.

3.

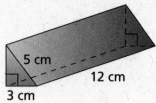

4.

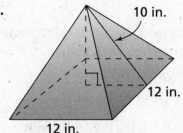

5.

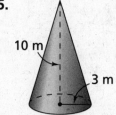

6.

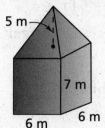

7. A cone and a square pyramid have the same volume and height.
   a. Both solids have volume 72 in.³. If the cone has radius 4 in., find the area of the base of the pyramid.
   b. If the base of the pyramid has side length 6 m, find the radius of the cone.

8. You can create an hourglass by placing two congruent cones inside a cylinder, as shown. Find the volume of space between the cones and the cylinder.

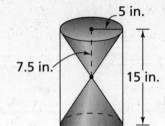

Additional Practice

1. A sphere has radius r. A plane slices the sphere at a distance h from the center of the sphere.
   a. Draw a diagram to represent the situation.
   b. Find the exact area of the circular cross section if $h = 3$ inches and $r = 5$ inches.
   c. Find the exact area of the circular cross section if $h = 8$ inches and $r = 17$ inches.

2. Suppose you double the radius of a sphere. Describe the effect this has on the volume of the sphere.

3. Compare the volumes of a sphere with radius of 3 cm and a hemisphere with radius of 6 cm.

4. A hollow plastic ball has outer radius 8 mm and inner radius 6 mm, as shown. Find the volume of the plastic needed to make the ball.

5. Use the figure of the sphere with given dimensions. The area of the shaded region is 225π in.^{2}.
   a. Find h.
   b. If you slice through the sphere at the shaded region, what is the volume of the slice and of the remaining sphere?

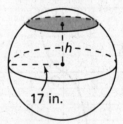

6. A farm silo consists of a cylinder with a hemisphere on top. Find the volume of a silo if the radius is 5 meters and the height of the cylinder portion is 20 meters.

7. The container shown below holds three tennis balls. Find the exact volume of space between the tennis balls and the container if the balls fit snugly.

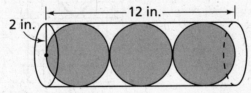

Find the volume of the shaded region.

8.

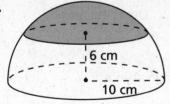

9.

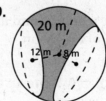

Name _____ Class _____ Date _____

Additional Practice

1. a. Reflect $\overline{AB}$ with endpoints $A(4, 5)$ and $B(0, 3)$ over the line with
   equation $y = -1$. Write the coordinates of the image.
   b. Reflect the image of $\overline{AB}$ over the line with equation $y = 2$. Write the
   coordinates of this new image.
   c. Describe a single transformation that maps $\overline{AB}$ onto the final image.

2. a. Reflect $\overline{AB}$ with endpoints $A(4, 5)$ and $B(0, 3)$ over the line with
   equation $x = 3$. Write the coordinates of the image.
   b. Reflect the image of $\overline{AB}$ over the line with equation $x = -1$. Write the
   coordinates of this new image.
   c. Describe a single transformation that maps $\overline{AB}$ onto the final image.

**For Exercises 3–6, decide whether each graph has any lines of symmetry.
Prove your conjecture.**

3. $y = x^3$

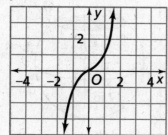

4. $y = \pm\sqrt{x - 2}$

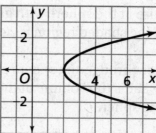

5. $y = \frac{1}{x}$

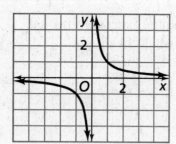

6. $y = |x + 3|$

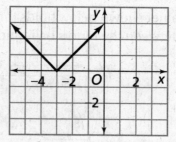

7. Suppose that you have point S and its reflection image S'. Describe how
   you can find the line of reflection.

8. Graph the line $x + 2y = 6$. Write an equation for its image after a
   reflection over the x-axis.

Additional Practice

1. a. Apply the rule $(x, y) \mapsto (x - 4, y + 3)$ to parallelogram $ABCD$ with vertices A(0, 0), B(2, 3), C(7, 3), and D(5, 0). Draw $ABCD$ and its image $A'B'C'D'$. Label all vertices.

   b. Describe how $A'B'C'D'$ relates to $ABCD$.

2. Use $\triangle ABC$ with vertices A(2, 3), B(5, 4), and C(3, 0).

   a. Reflect $\triangle ABC$ over the line $x = 2$ and label the vertices $A'B'C'$.

   b. Reflect $\triangle A'B'C'$ over the line $x = -3$ and label the new vertices $A''B''C''$.

   c. Find the coordinates of vertices $A'B'C'$ and $A''B''C''$.

   d. Is there a single mapping that sends $\triangle ABC$ onto $\triangle A''B''C''$? If so, describe it.

3. Use the circle with equation $x^2 + y^2 = 9$.

   a. Substitute $x + 4$ for x in the equation. Graph the result. Predict the result if you substitute $x - 4$.

   b. Substitute $y + 5$ for y in the equation. Graph the result. Predict the result if you substitute $y - 5$.

   c. Apply the rule $(x, y) \mapsto (x - 4, y - 5)$ to the points on the circle. Describe how your predictions differ from the mapping notation.

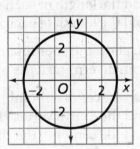

For Exercises 4–6, use geometry software or a pencil and paper. Copy each figure. Then find the image of the figure using the given counterclockwise rotation about point P.

4. 30°

5. 45°

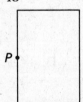

6. 120°

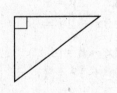

7. a. Use $\triangle ABC$. Draw the final image of $\triangle ABC$ reflected over lines ℓ and m.

   b. Fill in the blank: The composition of the reflections over intersecting lines is equivalent to a _____.

   c. Find the angle of rotation and mark the center of rotation.

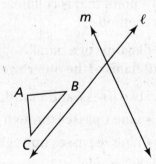

Name _____ Class _____ Date _____

Additional Practice

For Exercises 1 and 2, points A and B are endpoints of a diameter of a circle. Point C is the center of the circle. Find the length of the diameter and the coordinates of C.

1. $A(-9, 12)$, $B(17, 21)$
2. $A(-2x, 3y)$, $B(5x, -4y)$

3. One endpoint of a diameter of a circle is $(5, 12)$. The center of the circle is $(3, -5)$. Find the other endpoint of the diameter.

4. The vertices of parallelogram $ABCD$ are $A(1, -2)$, $B(3, 3)$, $C(9, 3)$, and $D(7, -2)$.
   a. Find the length of each side.
   b. Find the length of each diagonal.

5. If you know the coordinates of the vertices of two triangles, explain how you can determine if the triangles are congruent, rather than similar.

6. Three vertices of a rhombus are $M(3, 13)$, $A(0, 14)$, and $T(2, 16)$.
   a. Find the fourth vertex H.
   b. Find the center of the rhombus.

7. A segment has midpoint $(9, -12)$ and length 17. Give the coordinates for the endpoints of the segment in each case.
   a. The segment is on a horizontal line.
   b. The segment is on a vertical line.
   c. Give possible coordinates if the segment is neither horizontal nor vertical.

8. Which of the following pairs of lines are parallel? Explain.
   A. $3x - 2y = 8$
      $-3x + 2y = 9$
   B. $x + \frac{3}{2}y = 6$
      $2x - 6y = 12$
   C. $2x - 8 = 4$
      $5x + 12 = 17$
   D. $4x + y = 12$
      $-2x + \frac{1}{2}y = 14$

9. Find a point that is collinear with $J(3, -7)$ and $K(11, -5)$. Explain your method.

10. One diagonal of a parallelogram has endpoints $(3, -2)$ and $(8, 4)$. Give the coordinates of the other two vertices if the parallelogram is a rectangle.

11. Draw two lines ℓ and m with the following characteristics.
    • Line ℓ passes through $(0, 3)$ and $(-3, 0)$.
    • Line m passes through $(-4, 4)$ and $(4, 4)$.
    Find the coordinates of the point at which they intersect.

Name _____ Class _____ Date _____

Additional Practice

Lessons 7.8 and 7.9

Write an equation of a line perpendicular to the given line.

1. $2x - y = 12$

2. $x - 3y = 15$

3. $y = -4x + 5$

4. $x - 5 = 0$

5. $12x - 16y = 20$

Write an equation of the line through the given point and perpendicular to the given line.

6. $(0, 0); 2x - 3y = 12$

7. $(1, 4); x - 5y = 15$

8. $(0, -2); y = 2x + 5$

9. $(5, 6); y - 3 = 0$

10. $(4, 0); 5x - 10y = 20$

For Exercises 11–14, find the distance from the given point to the given line.

11. $(-1, 3)$; the line with equation $-3x - y = 9$

12. $(0, 6)$; the line with equation $4x - 5y = 20$

13. $(8, 5)$; the line through points $(4, 2)$ and $(-1, 5)$

14. $(2, -3)$; the line with equation $y = -3x + 6$

15. Imagine that a classroom is on a three-dimensional coordinate system, as shown below.

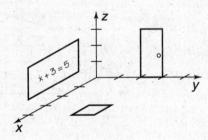

    a. Describe the location of the origin.
    b. Estimate the ordered triples of the four corners of the door.
    c. Estimate the ordered triples of the four corners of the desk. (Assume the desk has no height.)
    d. Estimate the ordered triples of the four corners of the whiteboard.

16. Find the midpoint of the segment with the given endpoints.
    a. $A(4, 0, 2)$ and $C(0, 6, 2)$
    b. $D(0, 0, 2)$ and $F(4, 6, 0)$
    c. $B(4, 6, 2)$ and $G(0, 6, 0)$

17. One of the vertices of a cube with side length 5 is $(0, 0, 0)$. What is the length of a diagonal of the cube?

CME Project • *Geometry Practice Workbook*
© Pearson Education, Inc. All rights reserved.

Additional Practice

1. Let $A(4, 6)$ and $B(9, 11)$. Find the head of a vector that starts at the origin, has the same direction as $\overrightarrow{AB}$, and is three times as long as $\overrightarrow{AB}$.

2. Let $P(2, 5)$ and $S(6, 9)$. Find the head of a vector that starts at $(3, -2)$ and is equivalent to the vector from P to S.

3. Decide whether each statement is *true* or *false*.
   a. $\overrightarrow{AB}$ and $\overrightarrow{CD}$ are congruent vectors if they have the same direction and length.
   b. $\overrightarrow{AB}$ is equivalent to $\overrightarrow{CD}$ if and only if $B - A = D - C$.

4. Let $J(3, 4)$, $K(5, 1)$, and $L = J + K$. Draw a picture of O, J, K, and L. Show that $OJ = KL$ and $OK = JL$.

5. For $T(4, 5)$ and $R(5, 8)$, locate each of the following.
   a. $T + R$ **b.** $T + 2R$ **c.** $T + 3R$
   d. $T + \frac{1}{2}R$ **e.** $T + \frac{1}{3}R$

6. Use the figure.
   a. Name the four vectors shown.
   b. Use the head-minus-tail method to show that $\overrightarrow{A(A + B)}$ is equivalent to $\overrightarrow{OB}$ and that $\overrightarrow{OA}$ is equivalent to $\overrightarrow{B(A + B)}$.

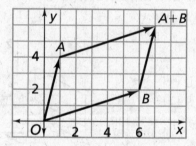

7. Let $J(1, 9)$ and $K(4, 12)$.
   a. Calculate head minus tail for $\overrightarrow{JK}$.
   b. Take $\overrightarrow{JK}$ anchored at the origin. Move it to $L(4, -3)$ by adding L to the head and to the tail. What are the coordinates of its new head and tail?

8. In the expressions below, capital letters are points, c, k, and x are constants, and O represents the origin. Classify each expression as a *point*, a *number*, or just plain *meaningless*.
   a. xA **b.** cO **c.** $A + C$
   d. $cB + A$ **e.** AD **f.** $kB - A$
   g. $x(GH)$ **h.** $B(k - A)$ **i.** $A(B - C)$
   j. $k(CD)$ **k.** $kX + cH$ **l.** $V(D + C)$

Additional Practice

1. Suppose $A(5, 6)$, $B(7, 9)$, $C(4, 6)$, and $D(8, 12)$. Prove that $\overleftrightarrow{AB} \parallel \overleftrightarrow{CD}$.

2. Let $A(4, 6)$ and $B(5, -3)$.
   a. Draw $\triangle OAB$.
   b. Find and label the coordinates of M, the midpoint of $\overrightarrow{OA}$, and N, the midpoint of $\overrightarrow{OB}$.
   c. Show that $\overline{MN} \parallel \overline{AB}$ and $MN = \frac{1}{2}AB$.

3. Let $A(-2, 5)$ and $B(4, 9)$.
   a. What multiple of $\overrightarrow{AB}$ has its head on the line $y = 4$?
   b. What multiple of $\overrightarrow{AB}$ has its head on the line $x = -1$?

4. Use the graph of point B and $\overrightarrow{OC}$. Find a vector equation of the line through B and parallel to $\overrightarrow{OC}$.

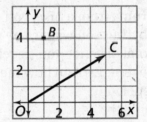

5. For $A(7, 10)$ and $B(4, 13)$, find C if B is the midpoint of $\overline{AC}$.

6. What point on $\overline{AB}$ is $\frac{2}{3}$ of the way from A to B?

7. a. Plot points $A(5, 2)$, $B(3, 6)$, and $C(8, 4)$ on the coordinate plane and connect them to form $\triangle ABC$.
   b. Translate $\triangle ABC$ to the origin by subtracting A from each vertex. Call the new vertices A_o (origin), B_o, and C_o. Find midpoints M, N, and K of sides $\overline{A_oB_o}$, $\overline{B_oC_o}$, and $\overline{A_oC_o}$, respectively.
   c. Write vector equations for $\overleftrightarrow{A_oN}$ and $\overleftrightarrow{B_oK}$. Do these lines intersect? If so, find the point of intersection.

8. Given $A(-5, 12)$, how can you find the coordinates of a point B, such that $\overrightarrow{OA} \perp \overrightarrow{OB}$?

9. Find a vector equation of a line through $A(3, 5)$ and perpendicular to $\overrightarrow{OA}$.

Additional Practice

1. You are docked in a motorboat on one bank of a river at A. You have to get gas across the river at B and then return the boat at C.

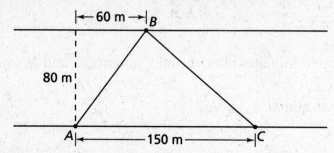

60 m
B
80 m
A   150 m   C

   a. Find the distance to the gas station.
   b. Find the total distance that you drive in this situation.
   c. Find a location for B on the opposite bank that minimizes the length of the path from A to B to C.

2. Returning from a hike, you see that your tent is on fire. A stream is nearby, but you want to be sure to get water at the spot that minimizes the total distance you travel from your current location, to the stream, to the tent. Explain how the reflection method helps you determine this spot.

3. Find the shortest path from $A(-6, 4)$, to any point P on the line with equation $-2x + 3y = 6$, to $B(-1, -2)$.
   a. Sketch a graph of the situation.
   b. What point P on the line $-2x + 3y = 6$ should the path go through? Explain.
   c. What is the length of the shortest path?

4. Find the shortest path from $A(-5, 3)$ to any point P on the line with equation $y = -3$, to $B(-1, -1)$.
   a. Sketch a graph of the situation
   b. What point P on the line $y = -3$ should the path go through? Explain.
   c. What is the length of the shortest path?

5. Line m has equation $y = 3x$.
   a. Points on line m are all of the form _____.
   b. Find a function that will give the distance between the point $(1, 3)$ and any point on m.
   c. For what value of x is this function at a minimum?

Additional Practice

1. For each of the following pool shots, locate the point you should aim for and sketch the path you expect the ball to take.

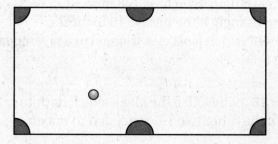

   a. Hit the ball off the top bumper and into the bottom right corner pocket.
   b. Hit the ball off the bottom bumper and into the top left corner pocket.
   c. Hit the ball off the top bumper, the bottom bumper, and into the top middle pocket.
   d. Hit the ball off the left bumper and into the top right corner pocket.

2. You are given line m and two points A and B that are not on the line. Describe a method for finding a point P on line m that minimizes the total length of the path from A to P to B.

3. A path on the coordinate plane must go from $A(5, 4)$ to point C on line ℓ with equation $x = 1$. Then the path goes to point D on line m with equation $x = 6$, and finally to $B(3, -4)$.
   a. Graph the shortest path.
   b. Find the coordinates of C and D.
   c. Suppose A is closer to line ℓ than to line m. Describe how the path from A to ℓ, to m, to B changes.

4. A path on the coordinate plane must go from $A(5, 4)$ to point C on line ℓ with equation $y = 2$. Then the path goes to point D on line m with equation $y = 7$, and finally to $B(-2, 4)$.
   a. Graph the shortest path.
   b. Find the coordinates of C and D.
   c. Suppose A is closer to line ℓ than to line m. Describe how the path from A to ℓ, to m, to B changes.

Additional Practice

1. The perimeter of an isosceles triangle is 24 inches.
   a. What is the area of the triangle if the base is 6 inches?
   b. What is the area of the triangle if the base is 8 inches?
   c. What is the area of the triangle if the base is 10 inches?
   d. Make a conjecture about which isosceles triangle of a given perimeter will enclose the most area.

2. A triangle has perimeter 18 inches. Use the given side length to determine the lengths of the other two sides needed to maximize the area.
   a. 6 inches
   b. 8 inches
   c. 10 inches
   d. Make a conjecture about the maximum area for this triangle.

3. Fill in the blank. The rectangle with the greatest area, given any perimeter, is a _____.

4. The perimeter of a rectangle is 40 cm and the length is 16 cm. What is the area of the rectangle?

5. A square and a rectangle have equal areas. The rectangle has a perimeter of 112.
   a. The length of the rectangle is 20. What is the perimeter of the square?
   b. If the area of the rectangle has been maximized, what is the perimeter of the square?

6. You have 30 feet of fencing to enclose a rectangular garden. You plan to use a stone wall for one side of the garden. The length of the stone wall is 16 feet. What size rectangle would maximize the area of the garden?

7. You have 100 feet of fencing to build a rectangular animal pen against a barn wall. Find the maximum area of the animal pen for each given length of the barn wall.
   a. 30 feet
   b. 40 feet
   c. 50 feet

8. Many triangles have side lengths 11 cm and 13 cm. Which of these triangles has the most area?

Additional Practice

Lesson 8.6

1. Describe a way to make a polygon with the same side lengths as the polygon in the figure, but with greater area.

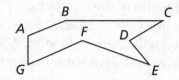

2. **a.** What type of parallelogram, with fixed perimeter, encloses the most area?
   b. What type of parallelogram encloses the most area if the side lengths are 12, 12, 24, and 24?

3. **a.** A quadrilateral has perimeter 40 meters. Prove that to maximize the area, the figure must be a square.
   b. A regular pentagon has perimeter 50 meters. Find the area of the pentagon.
   c. Show that an n-gon of a given perimeter must be regular to maximize the area it encloses.

4. A farmer has 300 meters of fencing to make a rectangular corral. A barn wall will border one length of the corral. The width of the corral is w.
   a. Express the length and the area of the corral in terms of w.
   b. What dimensions maximize the area of the corral?

5. **a.** Draw a rectangle.
   b. Construct a square with equal area.
   c. Compare their perimeters.

6. An equilateral triangle, a square, a regular hexagon, and a circle each have perimeter 30 meters.
   a. Find the side length (radius for the circle) and area of each figure.
   b. Make a conjecture about your results.

7. A rubber ball manufacturer wants to minimize costs on packaging. The company plans to package 1000 rubber balls, with diameters of 2 cm, in each box. What dimensions for the box minimize the amount of cardboard needed?

8. A pencil manufacturer wants to minimize costs on packaging. The company plans to package 20 pencils, with dimensions shown below, in each box. What dimensions for the box minimize the amount of cardboard needed?

8 mm ⬍ ◯)))))))▷ ────────── 190 mm ──────────▷

Additional Practice

1. Use the diagram of the soccer field.

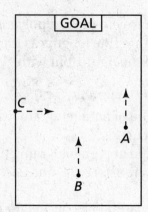

   a. Suppose you start at *A* and run toward the goal on the path indicated. Where along your path is the best location to take a shot? Label it *P*.

   b. Suppose you start at *B* and run toward the goal on the path indicated. Where along your path is the best location to take a shot? Label it *Q*.

   c. Suppose you start at *C* and run parallel to the goal line on the path indicated. Where along your path is the best location to take a shot? Label it *R*.

2. You are in a museum of natural history. There is a dinosaur skeleton on display. The skeleton sits on a platform that is 10 feet wide and 4 feet high. The skeleton is 20 feet tall. Your eye level is 5 feet. Sketch a picture of the situation. Then use your sketch to determine where you should stand for the maximum viewing angle.

3. A hockey player skates across the ice on the path indicated. At what point along the path should the player shoot at the goal?

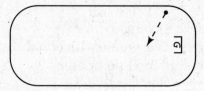

4. Suppose *A* is fixed in a plane. Function *f* determines all points in the plane that are equidistant to *A*.

   a. Make a contour plot for *f*.

   b. Label each contour line with the appropriate number.

   c. What shape is each contour?

5. Suppose $\overline{AC}$ is fixed in a plane. Function *g* determines a point's distance from $\overline{AC}$.

   a. Make a contour plot for *g*.

   b. What shape is each contour?

   c. How would the contours for *g* change if you look at all the points in space (not just in the plane)?

6. Suppose *C* and *D* are fixed in a plane. Function *f* is defined so that $f(A) = AC + 3AD$. Make an approximate contour plot for *f* by hand.

Additional Practice

1. Place two thumbtacks on a piece of cardboard. The thumbtacks represent the foci of an ellipse. Tie a string in a loop so that when you pull the loop taut, the loop is 5 inches long. Place the loop around the thumbtacks and around a pencil. Trace around the thumbtacks keeping the string taut. Explain why this method guarantees that you draw an ellipse.

2. A playground is surrounded by an elliptical walkway.

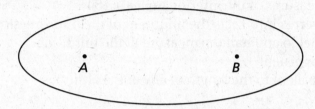

   Suppose that the swings are at A and the sandbox is at B. You walk from the swings, to the sandbox, to any point on the walkway. Then you walk back to the swings. Is there a point on the walkway that will minimize your total distance?

3. A builder uses ellipses to build a new building. The builder stacks the ellipse-shaped floors one on top of another so that the area of each floor decreases as the height of the building increases. Each floor is 10 feet tall and the building has 4 floors. Draw a contour plot of the building. Imagine you are looking down from the top.

4. You are on a camping trip and your tent catches on fire again. This time, your bucket is with your supplies. You must get the bucket, then get the water, and then put out the tent fire. Find the point along the river where you should go to minimize your path to put out the fire.

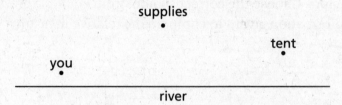

5. A city has two matching monuments with a road going between them. The city council wants to build a raised walkway to go over the road and both monuments. An engineer makes a plan that creates a path such that the sum of the distances between each monument and the walkway remains constant. Sketch a picture of what you believe the engineer has in mind.

Additional Practice

1. Use the given side length of an equilateral triangle. Find the sum of the distances from point A inside the triangle to the sides of the triangle.
   a. 12 cm   b. 20 m   c. 9 in.

2. For each property, list the type(s) of triangle(s), *equilateral*, *isosceles*, or *scalene*, that has the given property.
   a. The sum of the measures of the interior angles is 180°.
   b. The altitude at a vertex intersects the midpoint of the opposite side.
   c. A midline is parallel to and half the measure of the third side.
   d. Base angles are congruent.
   e. The height is equivalent to the length of any of the altitudes.

3. The vertices of a triangle are $A(-2, 4)$, $B(3, 4)$, and $C(0, 0)$.
   a. Classify the triangle as *equilateral*, *isosceles*, or *scalene*.
   b. Find the sum of the distances from $P(1, 3)$ to each side of the triangle.
   c. Find the height of the triangle.

4. A triangle has vertices $(-2, -2)$, $(3, 3)$, and $(6, 0)$. A function F is defined as the sum of the distances from point Q to the sides of the triangle.
   a. For $Q(3, 2)$, find the value of F.
   b. For what coordinates of Q does F have its least value?
   c. For what coordinates of Q does F have its greatest value? What is the greatest value of F?

5. Triangle JLK is right and isosceles, where $JL = LK$ and $\overline{JP}$, $\overline{LN}$, and $\overline{KM}$ are angle bisectors. Choose the correct symbol from $=$, $>$, $<$, or NG (not enough information given) to compare the relative measures of each given pair.
   a. JN _____ NK
   b. LM _____ LP
   c. JM _____ JN
   d. $KN + NL$ _____ $JN + NL$
   e. area of $\triangle JMK$ _____ area of $\triangle KPJ$
   f. $m\angle MOL$ _____ $m\angle POL$
   g. area of $\triangle JNL$ _____ area of $\triangle KNL$
   h. KM _____ KL
   i. LN _____ LK

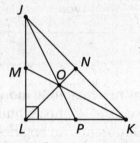